UNDESTANDING

YOUR

PASSION

1

ESANYE AYONMIKE

2

Dedication

I'm dedicating this book to God almighty for the gift of life and talents that he has bless me with. Secondly to my late father Capt. Emma Ayonmike, to my lovely mother Mrs. Julian Ayonmike and siblings who has been in support right from the time I started showing interest in writing.

To my spiritual parents Papa Ayo and Mama Helen Oritsejafor for their prayers and riche words upon the life of every members of Word of Life Bible Church.

And lastly to everyone out there that are discourage in one or two situation that they find their selves, I say keep holding on in every good things of life that you believe in and you will get there in Jesus name. Amen.

ESANYE AYONMIKE

3

4

INTRODUCTION

I have come across so many people that are still finding it difficult to define what they want from life. Many of them have tried so many things still they lack inner peace and fulfilment, because they cannot develop interest in the ideal job. They have to do a better one that will later develop into something that they have passion for.

◆ ◆ ◆

Some people cannot tell the difference between like, interest and passion, as they confuse what they feel at a particular point in time. 4

Having a job for the first time in four years after your graduation or after you lost a job, can make anyone take a job that in an ideal situation he/she will not apply for.

It's not bad though to start from somewhere, but what is bad is to remain in a particular job you have no passion or interest in, for a very long time without thinking of a change just because of the fear of the unknown.

Let the fear of your unknown give you your first step to start looking for the place of your interest, if you don't want to take the bold step to start looking for your place of passion with great speed.

5

CHAPTER ONE

What Is Your "Like or Likes"?

When this question first came into my mind, I was like what is my "like"? I asked myself what made me felt that I liked this or that. Also was I sure that my work was what I liked? Or I worked based on what other persons like about me? Or I did it because I couldn't tell the differences between doing it for myself or for the persons that were around me, just to please the person.

◆ ◆ ◆

So now let me ask you this, what is your like?

6

I will love you to give it some thought.

I know some people have different answers, if you do,

I will love you to list them down so you won't misplace it. You will need it!

According to the dictionary like is used to draw attention to the nature of an action or event.

When I was growing up I wanted to become a doctor, but when I entered into the secondary school (high school) I wanted to become an accountant because I used to assist my class teacher to prepare the profit and loss account, alongside the balance sheet for the next lesson.

could say I was among the best student in

the class then.

7

When I wrote my Western African Senior Secondary School Examination, I got F9 (fair) in accounting. I was angry! I dropped accounting and when I got into the university, I ended up studying Health, Safety and Environmental Education. Today I work in a TV station, don't ask me how?

◆ ◆ ◆

For I can only say it's the favour of God that made it possible. Any way I'm a movie producer, that's how I got the job as a broadcasting producer.

◆ ◆ ◆

You may have found out that you like or love something from the start but it's not working well for you. It does not mean that your first feeling is a new one, so don't stop there, you have to keep trying till you get a good result for it.

8

Let's look at how you can handle what you like to do or become. In some part of the world, some parents dictate what they want their children to become in life despite the dreams that the child has been developing while growing up.

Everything in life has a foundation especially when it concerns understanding your propose in life.

I will say the foundation is your "like or likes". Your "like" can build into interest which you can later grow into passion.

An important aspect about foundation is that you must be convinced that your "likes" are self-made decisions that you really want to do. You must understand it, because until you understand what you are about to do, you won't be able to develop it. So, start working on your "likes" today!

9

CHAPTER TWO

How To Develop Your
"Likes" Into Interest

As we see in the last chapter the dictionary definition of like, that of interest is the feeling of wanting to know or learn about something or someone.

On this chapter we'll be looking on the ways one can develop his or her" like". Most "likes" never get to the place of interest before they die.

10

There are several ways one can develop his/her" likes" if he or she can handle more than one.

After being able to identify your "likes" base on self-motives, the next thing you should be thinking of, is how you can get better in that thing that you like so much?

The understanding that you have built around what you like, will make it easier for you to start putting in place the steps you need to make it happen.

For instant, if your "like" is shoes, you can develop that" like" into interest by think-ing on how to create designs of shoes that are uniquely different. To start designing shoes, you need to start step by step devel-opment, thus:

11

1. Lean how to draw, if you don't know how to.

2. Know the meanings of colours so you can combine them effectively.

3. Practice on different designs often.

4. Learn several types of shoes and their unique functions.

5. Know the qualities and types of materials used to manufacture shoes.

In the processes of developments, don't belittle any aspect of learning. Frequent practices leads to creativity which builds your "likes" into interest.

To create your interest is just few steps from your "likes". It takes very few steps to kill that interest that you have built. Everyone in life needs food to survive that's how your interest also needs food to grow into passion.

12

For interest to grow into full flesh passion, the following are essential;

1. Steady reminder of what you want from that thing that you are interested in.

2. Always practicing the steps you have marked out and improve on them.

3. Also make research to see the latest trend on that thing and add your own ideals to make it more unique. Don't be a total copycat!

4. Check out for the mistake of others in same interest and work-out a solution.

5. Don't be afraid to learn something new because you don't want to fail. New things make you better and your falls can makes you stronger.

6. Keep investing till that interest becomes a passion; any laxity can lead your interest back to "like".

13

CHAPTER THREE

*Things That Sustain Inter-
est Into Passion*

O nce you are able to understand
what your heart wants and you
have inner peace that you can't
explain, understand that your interest is
not far from it. Passion is strong and
barely controllable emotion, so passion
and interest as it concerns career and
dream needs a sustaining force. It will be
rare to see anyone that will say he/she has
not lost interest in anything.

❖ ❖ ❖

14

Losing interest in something doesn't just come over night; it always has a starting point.

Some of the starting point is the kind of people you discuss your interest with. Every person cannot understand from your perspective, be it negativity or positivity. You are the one that has that vision, hold it on!

If people can't understand or support your vision, don't force them to. Why? Because the more you are trying to make them understand, the more some discourage you. It's your vision, start working on it till it becomes reality. Those who did not understand then will see

People with the mind set of possibility are the best set of people to discuss your ideas with especially if you have not gotten the full picture of what it's all about.

15

Your self-determination can also kill or lead your interest into passion.

No matter the encouraging or discouraging words you hear from people, maintain focus. How you use what you have heard to empower what you what to do will determine if you are growing or killing your dreams.

Note the following to keep your interest growing to the level of pouring all your passion into it:

1. After you identify your interest, keep working on it irrespective of failure. Keep working on it until you have the full knowledge of it. Starting small does not mean that you cannot grow in it.

2. Let your work towards be current. The more you procrastinate about it, the more the possibility of doing it will becomes slim. Everyone has a set-time of readiness, whenever they want to do something and they do not do it

at that set-time, it will be difficult for them to do it very well later, because they relaxed and lost the first burning drive.

3. Like I said earlier on, what you hear and listen to can make you or mar you.

4. For you to be able to keep your passion in your interest, you will have to sustain it with a positive mindset. Always think positively, it will help you drive the fear of impossibility.

5. Fear is a spirit that eliminates big dreams. To overcome your fears, you will have to fight it. See your fears as a stepping stone to your next goal by practicing how to win it patiently.

Just as you want to have a very good success story, that is how your dream wants a new face, so work it out!

17

CHAPTER FOUR

How Low Self-esteem Can
Kill Your Passion

I t's easy to destroy and complex to build. Just has the five factors listed in chapter four can help you build up a better passion, that's how it can also help you crumble your passion if you do not put them into practice efficiently.

◆ ◆ ◆

Another factor that can kill your career in speedily is low self-esteem.

18

Low self-esteem is when you always see yourself less in what you are doing, with the delusion that others are better than you.

In anything you do, there are people better than you. Some people permanently stop what they are interested in just because they lack the self-confident to face the competing market. In chapter three (3), I said fear is a spirit that kills big dreams. To overcome your fears, you have to fight it!

Low self-esteem is like your pizza and ice tea that goes hand in hand. Once fear crawls into what you are doing and you do not face it at the first stage, lack of self-worth will creep in and it can put you in a place where everything becomes challenging.

19

Low self-esteem is one deadly disease that you can fine in the career field because it can be transfer from one person to another unknowingly to the recipients of the disease. Once someone with low self-esteem sees everything as a challenge, he/she always look for someone to discuss the challenge with, and if your mindset is not positively incline you will start view things as challenge, and start hating people that are working their way through the challenge.

Don't see the failures at the back of your difficult stages instead; see the successes that wait you if you are able to pass that faze of your success. If you are finding it too difficult to work around it, look for someone with more experience in the field to help you out in it. Look for books and do research on how to build right self esteem.

20

Another way that you can fight it is to give it positive approach. Even though if everyone is seeing everything wrong with what you are doing, don't go into your shell to hid, come out strong in readiness to learn and improve yourself in what you are doing.

21

CHAPTER FIVE

*the Fight Between Inter-
est And Passion*

Some readers may ask in what way can interest conflict with passion. Some people don't actually no when they are fighting against their passion using their interest as an excuse.

This fight is normally common in an official environment, when leaders fight their subordinates that do things they love to do.

22

They have to go all out to make sure that their subordinate does not do the work,

so that they will not lose their position or job to their subordinate. This is where interest start fighting against passion.

◆ ◆ ◆

Anyone that has passion for something always give people chance to contribute their ideal to it without feeling intimidated about whoever does it.

◆ ◆ ◆

Interest can be so deadly if it doesn't give a chance to passion. Mishandling of interest can kill any career within a twinkle of an eye. Be careful with interest as it can easily give way for passion to die.

◆ ◆ ◆

Your passion in your interest does not have enough focus to bring success you desire in your career.

23

Careers are first birthed through interest and not passion.

Stop fighting with people excelling in your work place. It's alright to be so passionate about something but very wrong to allow your interest kill your career.

How To know When Interest Conflicts With Passion

1. When you are a job addict and deprive others from assisting you in your job.

2. When you are always angry or envious of anyone excelling in your area of passion.

3. When you always think that you can do it better.

4. When you reject corrections recurrently.

24

◆ ◆ ◆

How To Identify Diminishing Interest In Passion

Most people can't tell when they are losing interest in something they once loved, till they totally can't do anything about it anymore.

There are few ways for you to find out if you are losing interest in that thing that you were once passionate about:

◆ ◆ ◆

1. When you easily forget appointments about your area of interest.

25

2. Giving lesser attention to your area of interest.

3. When you frequently procrastinate.

Make Your Passion An
Unstoppable Force

Some people really don't see things from positive angles no matter how you present it. Don't hate them for it because their interest is not in it. No matter how you persuade them, it won't change their perspective. Most times the kind of people you discuss your passion with matters a lot. If you are discussing it with A and he/she is not interested, don't force him/her to so at the end of it, A will not discourage you out of it. It is your dream, if you want it to become reality, look for the right sources to channel it to.

26

Looking for the right sources simply means, looking for the right persons to discuss it with that can give you the step by step guidelines you need to develop that dream into reality.

Once you find your channel, maintain focus! There are several things you will encounter as you build your dreams that you will love to try. Try different things, but don't lose your focus! Focus is the only force that turns dreams into realities.

◆ ◆ ◆

Until you put your total mind in something, you can easily be distracted. No matter the level of your determination, if you do not work on your mind-set and how to be focus, you will total loose in life.

◆ ◆ ◆

27

So with your focus, determination and interest, your passion for your dream will become an unstoppable force.

◆ ◆ ◆

So many things have been said in this book, now how will you put your determination into play so that you can achieve your dream and grow passionately?

I will advise you to write it on some where you can see it every now and then.

28

by

Esanye Ayonmike